COLLINS

Best Walks
AROUND
INVERNESS

by Richard Hallewell

Illustrations by Rebecca Johnstone

HarperCollins*Publishers*

Published by Collins
An Imprint of HarperCollins*Publishers*
77-85 Fulham Palace Road
London W6 8JB

First published 1998

The walks in this guide were first published in
Bartholomew's *Walk Loch Ness and the Spey Valley.*

The landscape is changing all the time. While every care has
been taken in the preparation of this guide, the Publisher accepts
no responsibility whatsoever for any loss, damage, injury or
inconvenience sustained or caused as a result of using this guide.

Printed in Italy

ISBN 0 00 4487095

98/1/15.5

CONTENTS

Key map for the walks, key to map symbols							4
Introduction							5

Walk		Grade					Page
Walk 1	Inverness Islands	C	WC			🚌	10
Walk 2	Caledonian Canal	B	WC		🐾	🚌	11
Walk 3	Creag Phadrig	C			🐾	🚌	12
Walk 4	Reelig Glen	C			🐾		13
Walk 5	Culburnie	B					14
Walk 6	Dog Falls	B	WC		🐾		15
Walk 7	Loch Affric	A		🥾	🐾		16
Walk 8	Plodda Falls	C			🐾		17
Walk 9	Fort Augustus to Glen Moriston	A	WC	🥾		🚌	18
Walk 10	Inchnacardoch Forest	C			🐾	🚌	19
Walk 11	Foyers to Whitebridge	B	WC	🥾		🚌	20
Walk 12	Farigaig Forest	C	WC		🐾	🚌	21
Walk 13	Loch Duntelchaig	B		🥾			22
Walk 14	Strath Dearn	B		🥾			23
Walk 15	Brodie Castle	C	WC			🚌	24

Symbols

WC   Public conveniences available at route, or in nearby town. (NB: these facilities are often closed in winter.)

🥾   Hill walking equipment required. Strong boots; warm waterproof clothing; map and compass for hill routes.

🐾   Route suitable for dogs.

🚌   Public transport available to this route. Details given on individual routes.

Grade

A   Requires a high level of fitness and – for the hill routes – previous experience of hill walking. The use of a detailed map is advised.

B   Requires a reasonable level of fitness. Book map sufficient.

C   A simple, short walk on good paths.

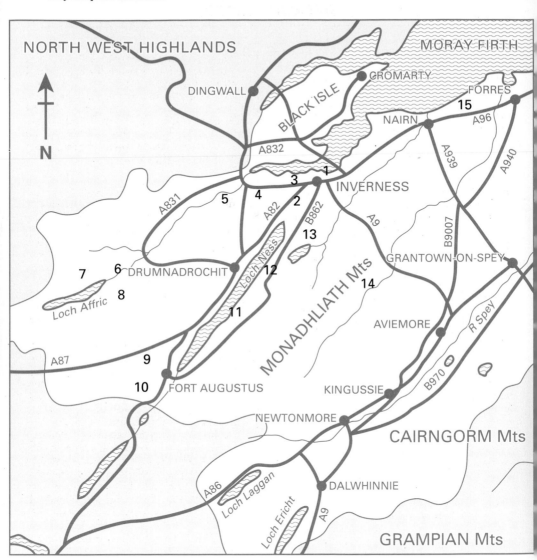

Key to map symbols

●●●	Route	✹ ✹	Marshland
——	Metalled Road	...::..::...	Moorland
++++++	Railway	♧ ♧	Coniferous Woodland
Ⓟ	Parking	♤ ♤	Broad-leaved Woodland
_i_	Information Centre	50m	Contour : shaded area is above height indicated
⌃	Viewpoint		

INTRODUCTION

ABOUT THIS BOOK

This is a book of walks, each of which can be completed within one day. Each route is graded according to its level of difficulty, and wherever specialist hill walking equipment is required this is specified. There is a description of each route, including information on the character and condition of the paths, and with a brief description of the major points of interest along the way. In addition there is a sketch map of the route. Car parks, where available, are indicated on the route maps. The availability of public conveniences and public transport on particular routes is listed on the contents page, and at the head of each route. The suitability or otherwise of the route for dogs is also indicated on the contents page. The location of each route within the area is shown on the key map, and a brief description of how to reach the walk from the nearest town is provided at the start of each walk. National grid references are provided on the maps. The use of a detailed map, in addition to this book, is advised on all grade A walks.

Before setting out, all walkers are asked to read through the section of Advice to Walkers at the end of the Introduction – it never pays to become lax in taking safety precautions.

THE AREA

(Numbers in italics refer to individual walks.)
At the peak of the ice age glaciers covered this entire area, with the exception of a few nunataks – mountain peaks which thrust up above the general level of the ice.

As the glaciers melted they became smaller and retreated into the higher hills, where the air was cold enough and precipitation high enough to maintain them. Even today, in the cooler north-facing corries of the high hills, drifts of snow linger well into the summer.

The glaciers, although reduced in size, continued to move down the valleys: generating ice in the high corries (bowl-shaped depressions in the hillside – common throughout the area) and slowly flowing downhill, until the air temperature was high enough to melt the ice.

The progress of the glaciers gave the valleys a broad, U-shaped cross-section. The deepest cuts made by the glaciers were along fault lines, where two plates of the Earth's crust meet, and where the rocks are already crushed and weakened. The major fault in the area is along the Great Glen, and it is no coincidence that here the ice excavated Scotland's deepest loch: Loch Ness (*10,11*), over 800ft (250m) deep in places. Other lochs in the area formed by glacial erosion include Loch Laggan, Loch Etricht and Loch Affric (*7*).

HISTORY

The first settlers arrived in the north around 8000 years ago. Around 2500 BC the first few Celts arrived; followed, around 600 BC, by more warlike groups of the same people. The Celts continued to arrive – not in concentrated attacks, but in small groups – throughout the next few centuries. They built large forts on easily defended hilltops. Examples of these forts are at Dun da Lamh; Farigaig, overlooking Loch Ness; Ord Hill, in the Black Isle; and Creag Phadrig (*3*), in Inverness.

The Romans had arrived in Britain in 78 AD, and quickly subjugated the south before moving north. The Roman Army marched up the east coast and, somewhere on the eastern fringe of the Grampians, between the River Tay and Inverness, fought a victorious battle against the combined forces of the northern hill tribes.

The Roman Army immediately withdrew, and made no further, serious, attempts to conquer the Highlands, preferring the expensive and inefficient alternative of building defensive walls across the breadth of the country (Hadrian's Wall in 122 AD; the Antonine Wall in 143 AD). Hadrian's Wall was finally overrun in 383 AD, and the Romans departed soon after.

The Pictish kingdom was a large and a powerful one, covering most of the Highlands – Inverness was a local capital – yet little remains as proof of the extent of their rule except a few place names and a collection of carved stones. These beautiful monuments are evidence of a distinctive and sophisticated national style, but they are cyphers, as obscure as their makers. They were produced between the 6th and the 9th centuries – a series of slabs, decorated with intermingled images; representational and abstract – and varying in content; pagan, Christian and secular.

In this area some of the best examples are the Rodney Stone at Brodie Castle (15), the stone at Rosemarkie Church, the Boar Stone at Knocknagael (2½ miles (4km) south of Inverness) and the giant Sueno's Stone at Forres – some 20ft (7m) high, and carved all over with images from some forgotten battle.

The name Scotland is derived from the Scots – a Celtic tribe who came from Ireland about 500 AD, and founded a small kingdom in Argyll, called Dalriada.

The most famous of the Scots was Columba, a churchman. In 565 AD he journeyed up the Great Glen to meet with Brude, King of the Picts, at Inverness. Columba had two main objectives in his embassage; firstly, to gain permission to send his acolytes throughout Pictland to establish religious foundations; and, secondly, to sue for peace for the Scots, to allow them to expand their territories. Columba was successful and from that moment the Gaelic, Latin and Christian culture of the Scots began to replace that of the Picts. The political unification of the two nations followed in 843 AD.

The move towards unity was accelerated by the attacks of the Vikings – who had begun to trouble both nations from around 800 AD – and was sealed by a peculiarity of Pictish law: the descent of power was matrilineal. This meant that the successor to a king would not be his son, but his sister's son, or his daughter's son; thus, when the Pictish King's daughter married the Scottish King, Alpin, the resulting son, Kenneth, was heir to the crowns of both kingdoms, which he duly inherited.

The Vikings colonised the north of Scotland and the islands, but in this area they never moved south of the Black Isle in any numbers.

By the time King Malcolm II died in 1034, Scotland was, in extent, largely as it is today. Prior to his death, however, he broke with the Celtic tradition of tanistry – whereby the crown was passed between various branches of the royal family – and gave the crown to his daughter's son, Duncan. There was considerable displeasure among the nobles who considered themselves the rightful claimants. MacBeth – who had a castle at Inverness – defeated Duncan, somewhere in Moray or the Black Isle, and killed him. He ruled Scotland (or, as the Gaelic-speakers called it, Alba) for 17 years, before he himself was killed by Duncan's son, Malcolm Ceann Mor (Great leader) – a man brought up in England, who brought with him many Anglo-Saxon followers, with their feudal culture and laws.

The importance of this episode was that it marked the end of the Celtic royalty of Alba, and the start of the Anglo-Norman kingship of Scotland. The Scottish kings now represented a minority in the kingdom, and, as a result, did not have the power to intimidate either the Celtic Highlanders, who continued to live much as they always had, or the Scottish nobles, who, by creating an alliance with anyone – French, English or Highland – could create havoc in this small, politically unbalanced country.

In the centuries following Duncan's accession, the politics of the area degenerated into local power struggles. The War of Independence, which climaxed with Bruce's victory of Edward II of England at Bannockburn, in 1314, was treated by most of the Celtic families as an opportunity to gamble for gain. Most of the clans prominent in this area in later years came out for Bruce at Bannockburn.

In 1371 Bruce's line failed, and the Stewarts came to power – the policies which they followed in the Highlands were frequently heavy-handed, but the Stewarts had considerable Highland blood, and seemed genuinely interested in the north. All the Stewarts, up to Mary, Queen of Scots, spoke Gaelic fluently, and remained proud of their Celtic ancestry.

It was during this period that the clan system reached its zenith. The system was the direct descendant of the tribal divisions of the Celtic race, common, at one time, throughout central Europe. Clann means children, but clan membership was always more flexible than that, with various families and individuals willing to give allegiance to a local chief for the safety of living within a group.

A chief might reckon his wealth in men, but his finances depended on cattle. Cattle raids were a central part of Highland culture, and so were the summer and autumn cattle drives. Each year great herds of fattened beasts were driven through the hills to the lowland markets. Some of the routes in this book follow the rough tracks they used, through narrow glens and across hill passes (7,9).

In 1603, James VI became King of both Scotland and England. In the wars which coloured the reigns of the last of the Stewarts (James, Charles I, Charles II and James VI and II), the north saw much of the action. Graham of Montrose, the finest general ever to lead a

Highland army, won a sequence of dazzling victories for the Catholic Charles I against the presbyterian Covenanters; and Graham of Claverhouse – Bonnie Dundee – was victorious for James VII at Killiecrankie. These were wars of religious ideology, but, however committed their generals were to the cause, the clans were committed only to profit and revenge. They watched to see which side their enemies joined, and joined the other.

In 1707 the Treaty of Union joined the parliaments of Scotland and England. In an independent Scotland the Highlands had been an area of considerable, ungovernable power; in the context of Great Britain it was simply a troublesome province.

By 1715 the clans were in rebellion, partly for the restoration of a Catholic, Stewart monarch (William and Mary had taken the throne of James VII in 1689) and partly in protest against the Union. The 1715 rebellion was a shambles, and, following its disintegration, General Wade was sent north from England to supervise the pacification of the Highlands. This he did, partly by raising regiments from the local population – more suited to the warfare of the terrain than were his own troops – and partly by building the first planned roads in the Highlands. These roads connected a series of forts, including Ruthven Barracks, Fort William, Fort Augustus and Fort George, at Inverness.

General Wade's Road is a common phrase on Highland maps: either alongside later, motor-roads, which have followed his original routes, or by the steep, hill tracks, now used only by hill walkers.

There was a second Jacobite rising in 1745. In all, only 6000 Highlanders joined the Stewart cause, but all the clans, Jacobite and Hanoverian alike, were punished in the aftermath of a battle which ended not only the rebellion, but also the power of the clans – Culloden.

The hardships endured by the Highlanders at the hands of the victorious Hanoverian army, were compounded by the insults of the ensuing legislation. Not only was the Disarming Act – first introduced after the 1715 rebellion – reinforced, but the people were banned from wearing the Highland tartans, under the threat of deportation.

Following Culloden, many of the clan chiefs, needing to establish themselves under the new regime, raised regiments from their clansmen, to fight for the Hanoverians. These regiments acquitted themselves with great bravery, and disproportionate loss, in Europe and America. The clan chiefs, now deprived of their ancient powers and responsibilities and little more than landlords of vast, unprofitable estates, had need more for money than for men.

All the Highland towns are products of this period: clearance towns, built to take the overspill when the glens were cleared of men and cattle to make way for sheep – more profitable tenants of the land.

Many Highlanders, unwilling to accept the new conditions, and often financially encouraged by their chiefs, emigrated. Others, not wishing to leave the country, moved to the new harbours along the coast, took jobs building the roads and railways or – at the start of the 19th century – Telford's Caledonian Canal (2).

The suppression of the spirit of the remaining Highlanders was so swift and successful that, within a hundred years of Culloden, the Highlands were safe enough to have become fashionable.

The transformation was largely triggered by a gradual appreciation of the bravery and effectiveness of the Highland regiments, and also by the work of James Ossian MacPherson – the successful perpetrator of one of the finest literary frauds of all time. In 1760 MacPherson published his first translations of ancient Gaelic epics, originally written by the 3rd-century bard, Ossian. MacPherson's epics, in their turgid, hollow English, were all his own work and were extraordinarily popular.

The romanticising of the Highlands was completed by Queen Victoria and Prince Albert, who purchased Balmoral Castle, in Deeside, in 1852. They started a vogue for Highland holidays which led directly to the development of the north-south rail links and the growth of the towns along the lines.

NATURAL HISTORY

The area can usefully be divided into a number of distinct environments, which recur along the various routes in this book – **native caledonian pine forest, commercial forestry, native broad-leaved woodland, mountain and moorland, farmland, freshwater**.

Caledonian pine forest (6,7). The **Scots pine** is the only obvious conifer indigenous to the British Isles. Forests containing this species, along with native broad-leaved woodland including **birch, oak, rowan, alder, willow** and **ash**, once covered much of the Scottish Highlands. Today the native forest exists only in a few small, protected pockets – in this area around the Cairngorms in the south, and in Glen Affric in the west.

A typical Caledonian pine forest consists almost entirely of the one species of tree, interspersed with **birch, rowan** and **alder**. Birch is particularly common in the damp conditions of Glen Affric.

Beneath the trees is a thick mat of **bell** and **ling heather, blaeberry, cowberry** and various mosses. In the Speyside forests there is also considerable **juniper** – a dark springy shrub which can grow in low thickets, or as a single plant, up to 25ft (7.5m) in height.

The forest contains a wide array of the smaller birds: **blue, great coal tits, treecreeper, bullfinch, chaffinch** and **wren**, as well as the more particular **goldcrest** and **siskin**, and the localised conifer specialists: **crested tit** and **Scottish crossbill**.

Of the larger birds, the most spectacular is the **capercaillie** – the largest of the native grouse. The cock is large, black and not unlike a turkey; but it is more likely to be heard, crashing through the branches of trees, than seen.

There is not a great deal of animal life peculiar to the forest, but **roe** and **red deer** are likely to be seen. **Red squirrels** are common in this area. Of the carnivores, **fox, badger, stoat, wildcat, otter** and **weasel** all inhabit the forest. The **pine marten**, once nearly extinct but now expanding in number and range, lives in both native and commercial forests (6,7).

Commercial forestry (3,4,8,9,10,12,13,15). Of major interest is the variety of conifer types which are now planted. The list includes **Scots pine; Sitka** and **Norway spruce; Japanese, European** and **hybrid larch; Douglas fir; western red hemlock** and a great many others. Most of the routes listed above pass through entirely commercial plantations, but in some the conifers are older, and widely spaced. These are maintained as beauty spots (4,8,12).

Mountains and moorland (7,9,13). The Highlands are famous for their moors: vast areas of **heather** which give a purple shade to the hillsides from July to September.

Flat areas of moorland are often floating on a considerable depth of peat, and pools of dark water often develop. These encourage plants such as **bog cotton, bog asphodel** and the pungent **bog myrtle**. For the most part, however, the moors are predominantly of **ling heather**, with **bell heather, blaeberry** and other shrubs intermixed. On the mountain slopes the **ling** gives way to a covering of **blaeberry, crowberry, dwarf juniper** and others.

Parts of the moor are burnt in the spring to encourage new growth in the heather to feed the **red grouse** – common up to 3000ft (900m). Other birds to be seen on the lower moors include the **skylark, stonechat, wheatear** and **curlew**. Crows are present: both the **carrion** and the grey cowled **hooded crow**.

The **red deer** are high in the hills during the summer, but return to the lower moors in the autumn, and can often be seen from the main roads during the winter. **Wildcat, fox** and **stoat** are present, although generally unseen, along with the **blue hare** which, like the **stoat**, turns white during the winter months.

One creature which existed in Scotland until the 9th century – the **reindeer** – has been reintroduced to the Cairngorms. They are quite tame and harmless.

The commonest of the birds of prey throughout the area is the **buzzard**, but there is always a chance of seeing a **kestrel, peregrine** or **merlin** on the moors; or even, in the more remote glens, a **golden eagle**.

Farmland (5,14). Farmland around the Moray Firth is varied and wildlife tends to consist of overspills from woodland reservoirs. Most of the woodland birds previously mentioned are present, along with the **robin, yellowhammer** and **greenfinch**. In addition there are **curlew, oystercatcher** and **lapwing** on the rougher pasture, and large flocks of **redwing** and **fieldfare** during the autumn and winter. Farm animals apart, the mammals tend to be small: **voles, bats, mice** and **shrews, stoat** and **weasel**. Flowers in the ditches, hedgerow, pastureland and woodland are abundant and varied.

Freshwater (1,2,4,10,15). The **bog cotton, asphodel** and **myrtle** and various mosses of the peat bogs give way to largely woodland plants as the small burns pass through their high-sided, narrow glens (4,8). Various pondweeds, reeds, sedges and grasses are common by the lochs and lochans, along with **water lily, water lobelia** and others.

The most famous of Scottish water birds – the **osprey** – nests in this area. This splendid bird is no longer as rare as it once was, and can be seen fishing at many of the lochs throughout the area.

Duck are very common at all stages of the rivers' development, with **mallard** and **teal** as high as the moor's edge, and **wigeon, pochard, goldeneye, red-breasted merganser, tufted duck** and **goosander** in the lower waters.

Also by the upper waters are **redshank, curlew** and **lapwing**; while **dippers** and **grey** and **pied wagtails** are common in the shaded dens (4,8).

None of the routes in this book passes close to the nesting areas of the **red-throated** or **black-throated diver** – the high lochans, specifically chose for their isolation – but both species nest within this area, and may be seen flying overhead.

The variety of freshwater fish in the area is not great. The most common of all is the **brown trout** – and the most important is the **Atlantic salmon**, which ascends the rivers during the summer, to spawn in the headwaters at the end of the year. In the lochs there are **pike** and **perch** in great numbers, **eels** and, in the deeper lochs, **char** – a distant cousin of the **salmon**.

There are few mammals which specifically live by the water, but one – the **otter** – is not uncommon throughout the area, although it is quite rare to see one. Other swimmers include **water vole** and **mink**.

There is one poisonous snake in the area – the **adder**. It is rare to see one – usually coiled in a patch of sunlight, somewhere quiet – and even rarer to be bitten. **Adders** are extremely shy and will always move if they sense anyone approaching. Anyone who is bitten should consult a doctor. Bites are not lethal, but they give rise to an unpleasant, temporary illness.

Two insects are deserving of note. The **cleg**, or **horse fly**, is very common, particularly in moorland areas, and delivers an irritating bite. Even more numerous, and the bane of the outdoor enthusiast's life, is the **midge**. These diminutive insects tend to congregate around water and are particularly active around sunset.

ADVICE TO WALKERS

Always check the weather forecast before setting off on the longer walks and prepare yourself for the walk accordingly. Remember that an excess of sunshine – causing sunburn or dehydration – can be just as debilitating as snow or rain, and carry adequate cover for your body in all conditions when on the hills.

Snow cover on higher slopes often remains well into the summer and should be avoided by inexperienced walkers as it often covers hidden watercourses and other pitfalls which are likely to cause injury. Also soft snow is extremely gruelling to cross and can sap energy quickly. Walking on snow-covered hills should not be attempted without an ice axe and crampons.

The other weather-associated danger on the hills is the mist, which can appear very swiftly and cut visibility to a few yards. A map and compass should always be carried while on the higher hills.

Obviously these problems are unlikely to arise on the shorter, simpler routes, but it is always wise when out walking to anticipate the worst and to be ready for it. The extra equipment may never be needed, but it is worth taking anyway, just in case. Spare food, a first aid kit, a whistle and a torch with a spare battery should be carried on all hill walks. In addition, details of your route and expected time of return should be left with someone, who you should advise on your safe return.

From August onwards there is grouse shooting and deer stalking on the moors. If you are undertaking one of the hill routes, first check with the local estate or tourist office, thereby avoiding a nuisance for the sportsmen and possible danger to yourself.

COUNTRY CODE

All walkers, when leaving public roads to pass through farmland, forestry or moorland, should respect the interests of those whose livelihood depends on the land. Carelessness can easily cause damage. You are therefore urged to follow the Country Code:

Guard against all risk of fire.

Keep all dogs under proper control (especially during the lambing season – April and May).

Fasten all gates.

Keep to the paths across farmland.

Avoid damaging fences, hedges and walls.

Leave no litter.

Safeguard water supplies.

Protect wildlife, wild plants and trees.

Go carefully on country roads.

Respect the life of the countryside.

1 Inverness Islands

Length: 2 miles (3km)
Height climbed: None
Grade: C
Public conveniences: Inverness
Public transport: Regular bus and train services
to Inverness from every direction

*A short walk along the banks of the River
Ness, in Inverness, including a path across
a small group of wooded islands.*

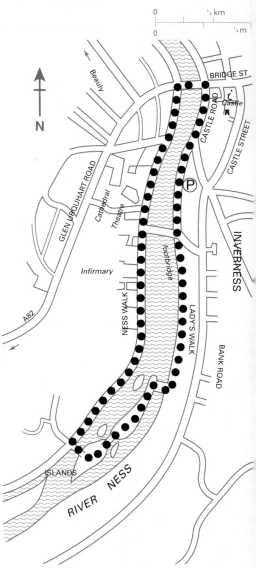

For some time Inverness has prospered as the
administrative centre for the remote country of the
north and west. It was the area's Pictish capital
when St Columba visited King Brude here in AD
565. However, the site was inhabited long before
that and has remained so, with increasing
importance, ever since. Inverness is now the home
of the administrative offices of the largest of
Britain's regions — Highland. The headquarters
of the Highlands and Islands Development Board
are also here.

The centrepiece of the town is the winding,
grass-banked River Ness, with its pedestrian
suspension bridges and wooded islands — this is
much the prettiest part of the town. Start walking
at the junction of Bridge Street and Castle Road.
Along this first stretch Inverness Castle sits on the
hill to the left of the path. This neat but rather
uninspiring building — the most recent of many
on the site — was completed in 1846 to replace
the castle destroyed by the Jacobites in 1746. It
houses administrative offices.

The way continues along Ness Bank and Lady's
Walk to the first of the islands. There are two
large islands, with a number of smaller ones
scattered around them. They are quiet, pleasant
parks, with a wide variety of tree types, and are
connected to each other, and to the banks of the
river, by a series of suspension footbridges.

Walk back along the west bank, beside Ness
Walk, past the modern Eden Court Theatre, and St
Mary's Episcopal Cathedral (1878). The latter
was the masterpiece of the local architect
Alexander Ross.

Turn right across the bridge, to return to the
starting point.

2 Caledonian Canal

Length: Up to 10 miles (16km)
Height climbed: None
Grade: C
Public convenience: Inverness
Public transport: Bus and train services to
Inverness from every direction

*A long flat walk by the side of the canal,
through woodland, farmland and residential
areas along the banks.*

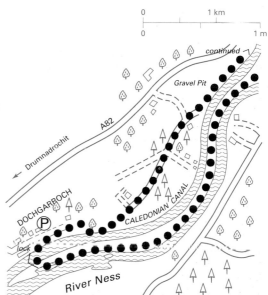

The Caledonian Canal was surveyed by Thomas
Telford and built in the early 19th century, with
the aim of eliminating the long and hazardous sea
trip round the north coast of Scotland. It runs 60
miles (100km), from Inverness on the North Sea
to Fort William on an arm of the Atlantic,
following the line of the Great Glen: a natural
furrow stretching from coast to coast along a fault
line. 22 miles of this distance is covered by the
canal; the balance through the lochs of Dochfour,
Ness, Oich and Lochy. This route follows the
canal from the Muirtown Basin to the last lock
before Loch Ness, at Dochgarroch.

Muirtown Basin is the assembly point for ships
waiting to pass through the swingbridge of the
A862 and on into the canal. There are always
boats to be seen here, tied to the wharf.

Across the road are the first four locks. The

canal has 28 altogether, lifting the ships to a
height of 106ft (32m) above sea level at Loch
Oich.

The path continues, past residential areas and
the picturesque hill of the Tomnahuirich cemetery,
to the bridge carrying the A82.

The road to the left here leads back into the
centre of Inverness. The one directly opposite
eventually joins up with the 'Inverness Islands'
route *(1)*. For the longer route continue by the
canal side. The path now runs along a narrow,
wooded strip of land between the canal and the
River Ness.

It is approximately 3½ miles (5.5km) from the
A82 to Dochgarroch. The path back, along the
north side, leaves the canal at the end of a small
wood (see map), rejoining it 1½ miles (2.5km)
further on and continuing to the A82 bridge.

11

3 Creag Phadrig

Length: 1 mile (1.5km)
Height climbed: 150ft (70m)
Grade: C
Public conveniences: Inverness
Public transport: Bus and train services to Inverness from every direction

A short hill walk through mixed woodland to an old hill fort. Very fine views and good paths.

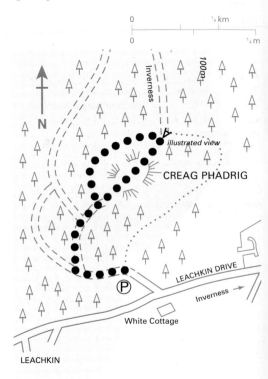

The fort on Creag Phadrig — its stone walls fused by heat — was probably built over 2000 years ago. Very little of the structure — 260ft (80m) long by 90ft (25m) wide — can now be seen, except the grass mounds which have grown over the walls, but it is a pleasant walk, through a mature forest of spruce, fir, larch and pine, and the views are excellent.

To reach the walk from Inverness, take the Beauly road, over the Caledonian Canal, and turn left up King Brude Road. Carry straight on at the roundabout, up Leachkin Road. Turn right on the road signposted to Blackpark. The car park is on the right, just opposite a white cottage — 2 miles (3km) from the town centre.

The creag is in clear view, and the path to the summit is well marked. Near the top it becomes steep, but the going is never difficult. The path approaches the fort from the west and leaves it to the east, leading down to an excellent viewpoint (see below) before cutting round the hill to the left and rejoining the original path.

An alternative return route is to follow the path down the north slope; turning right at the bottom to reach King Brude Road.

1. *Ben Wyvis* **2.** *Beauly Firth* **3.** *The Black Isle* **4.** *Ord Hill* **5.** *Chanonry Point* **6.** *Moray Firth* **7.** *Kessock Bridge* **8.** *Fort George* **9.** *Firth of Inverness* **10.** *Inverness*

4 Reelig Glen

Length: 1½ miles (2.5km)
Height climbed: 200ft (60m)
Grade: C
Public conveniences: None
Public transport: None

A number of routes through mature mixed woodland, with particularly fine conifers. Paths good.

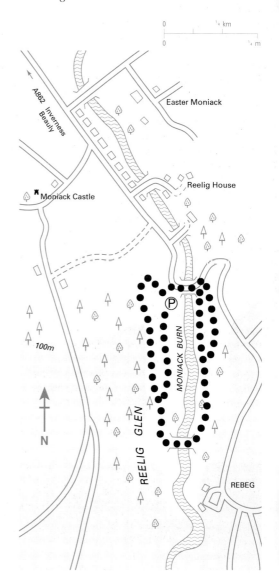

Reelig Glen lies some eight miles west of Inverness to the south of the A862 road to Beauly. Turn off this road and follow the signs for Moniack. Then, at the junction where Moniack Castle appears to the right, carry straight on, on the road signposted to Rebeg.

Reelig Glen was once — in common with so much of this corner of the country — the property of a branch of the Fraser family. It was sold to the Forestry Commission in 1949 for preservation and commercial development.

The glen was designed as a wooded, 'natural' garden, using many of the imported trees which are now associated with commercial forestry: Douglas fir, western red hemlock, Norway and Sitka spruce. The particular charm of this area is that the trees were planted so long ago (the glen was largely planned and planted by James Baillie Fraser, a writer and traveller, in the early 19th century) that they have attained a maturity which one rarely sees in Britain.

There are a number of paths through the glen, leading as far as a bridge over the burn, beside which are the ruins of a grotto — a common feature of planned gardens of the period. A leaflet is available from tourist and Forestry Commission offices which describes two particular routes, and provides a commentary on the points of interest along the way.

At one point, from the edge of the glen, there is a view across the surrounding countryside, including the Beauly Firth and Moniack Castle: a Fraser stronghold, now run as a winery.

5 Culburnie

Length: 5 miles (8km)
Height climbed: Negligible
Grade: B
Public conveniences: None
Public transport: None

An easy circuit on quiet, metalled, public roads, with views of the Beauly Firth and the surrounding farmland.

There is no particular reason why this road should be preferred to any other in the district. It is included as an example of one of the many pleasant minor roads in this low-lying V of land around the Beauly Firth, confined by the surrounding Highlands: from Inverness to Beauly — the Aird — and north-east into the Black Isle. This is an area of farmland and backroads and there are many walks to be found, with the aid of a detailed map.

To reach this route — from Inverness — take the A862 road towards Beauly, turning on to the A831 at the junction, and then taking the first turn to the left. Parking is available at the Lovat Mineral Water Visitor Centre at Fanellan which is well signposted from the bridge over the River Beauly.

The section of the route from Hughton to Kiltarlity Cottage provides the best views, across the farmland to the Beauly Firth, and south to the hills above Loch Ness. Here the road is lined with dykes and oak trees.

Beyond the junction there are fine views of the steep river valley, and of the towers of Beaufort Castle, largely hidden by trees. The castle was built for Fraser of Lovat in 1880, the previous building on the site having been destroyed by the Duke of Cumberland in the aftermath of Culloden in 1746.

Beyond the castle the road continues through a mixture of farmland and woodland. Keep right at the turn off for Kiltarlity and straight oon at the turn for Lonbuie to return to Hughton. Be adventurous though — the roads which radiate from this central circuit are all worth exploring. The route to Eskdale up the Beauly valley is particularly beautiful.

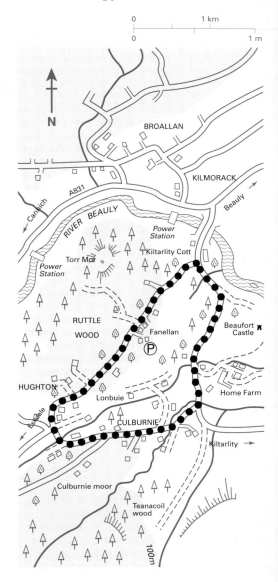

14

6 Dog Falls

Length: 4 miles (6.5km)
Height climbed: 350ft (100m)
Grade: B
Public conveniences: Car park
Public transport: None

A signposted trail through Scots pine forest, maintained in its natural state by the Forestry Commission. Path good.

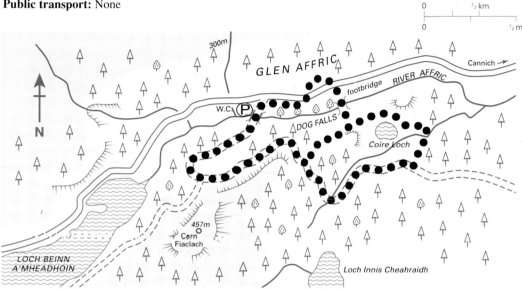

Due to climatic changes and excessive grazing and felling, the original Caledonian Pine Forest has been reduced to a few small pockets throughout the Highlands. Now, particularly around the Cairngorms and here, in Glen Affric, efforts are being made to encourage the forest to regenerate naturally.

To reach Glen Affric from Inverness, take the A862 towards Beauly, turning on to the A831 for Cannich at the junction. Turn right at Cannich on the Glen Affric road. The car park for Dog Falls is about 4 miles (6.5km) up this road.

The walk, which is clearly signposted, leads across a bridge over the River Affric and up the hill. After a short climb the path reaches a point where the hill nudges out of its tree cover for a moment and there is a fine view of the glen, and of the peaks on the far side. The loch below, to

the left, is Loch Beinn a' Mheadhoin, which has been dammed for hydro-electricity.

A little further on the path splits. The shorter route cuts down to the left, and the longer continues to Coire Loch — a small, round, green lochan fringed with peat bogs and mosses and surrounded by the pines. Climb the rocky outcrop beyond the loch and then continue along the path, down to the stile and a second footbridge over the river, just below the falls.

The route crosses the road and continues through the regular ranks of commercial forestry, and then recrosses the road and returns to the car park.

The woods of Glen Affric are inhabited by one of Britain's rarest mammals — the pine marten. They are very reclusive, but there is always the chance of seeing one.

7 Loch Affric

Length: 10 miles (16km)
Height climbed: None
Grade: A
Public conveniences: None
Public transport: None

A long walk on rough paths and Forestry Commission tracks, across moorland between Loch Affric and the surrounding hills, scattered with stands of Scots pine.

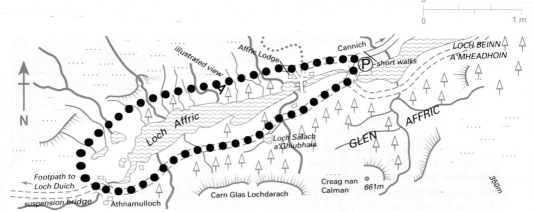

A metalled road leads for 7 miles (11.3km) from the Dog Falls car park *(6)* to the River Affric car park.

This is a lovely walk, between the steep hills and the loch, with the stands of pine by the water's edge. There is no difficulty with the route. On the north side of the loch it passes to the right of Affric Lodge, through a gate, and on across moorland. The path is rough and damp, but clear enough.

At the west end of the loch the path splits. To the right is the start of the long footpath to Loch Duich in Kintail on the west coast. Keep left here, across a bridge, past the cottage at Athnamulloch and across the floor of the glen to join the forestry track along the south side of the loch, back to the car park. Keep a look out for red deer along this route — particularly during the colder months.

There are two other short walks, along signposted routes, from the car park.

1. *Carn Glas Lochdaroch (771m)* **2.** *Carn a' choire Ghairbh* **3.** *Garbh Leac (1120m)*
4. *Mullach Fraoch-Choire (1102m)* **5.** *Ciste Dubh (982m)* **6.** *Loch Affric* **7.** *Bienn Fhada (1032m)*
8. *Creag a' Chaorainn* **9.** *Au Tudair* **10.** *Sguur na Lapaich*

8 Plodda Falls

Length: 1¹/₂ miles (2.5km)
Height climbed: 200ft (60m)
Grade: C
Public conveniences: None
Public transport: None

A short walk through mature conifer forest to a spectacular waterfall. Paths good, but damp in places.

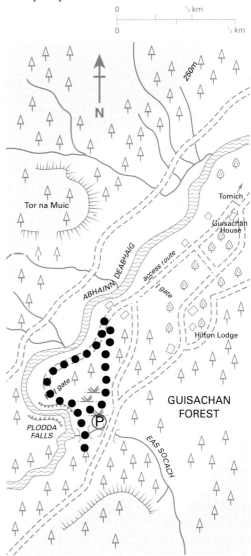

This short route is one for lovers of waterfalls. In a steep rocky gorge, overhung with vast conifer, the Eas Socach drops over 70ft (20m) into a pool swelled by the Abhainn Deabhag, which joins the burn of the falls at this point.

The village of Cannich is in Strathglass, on the A831 between Drumnadrochit and Beauly. Just across the river from Cannich a small road branches off the A831, signposted to Tomich. Just beyond Tomich the road forks. Shortly after the fork you will leave the metalled road and be on forest roads. You will come to a number of road junctions, but keep following the signs and you will arrive at Plodda Falls car park.

From the car park follow the forest walk downhill for approximately 350m and you will arrive at an old cast iron bridge. The bridge was built when Plodda was part of Guisachan Estate and owned at the time by Lord Tweedmouth. The bridge allows you a magnificent view over the top of the falls. Continue down the path where you will find several viewpoints looking up into the falls. The path divides further down the hill and you have the choice of taking a short route back to the car park or continuing downhill on a longer route.

The longer route takes you down on to a forest road with vast conifer (Douglas fir) forming a magnificent avenue. These conifers were planted round about 1900 and are being left to grow into majestic specimens. It was from these giants that in 1988 two trees were specially selected and cut to provide new masts for the *Discovery* which Scott sailed on his epic voyage to the Antarctic.

9 Fort Augustus to Glen Moriston

Length: 7 miles (11km) one way
Height climbed: 1200ft (360m)
Grade: A
Public conveniences: Fort Augustus
Public transport: Bus services from Inverness
stopping at Invermoriston and Fort Augustus

*A steep hill crossing, through forestry and
across moorland, on an old military road.
Very damp, and some athleticism is
required when crossing burns.*

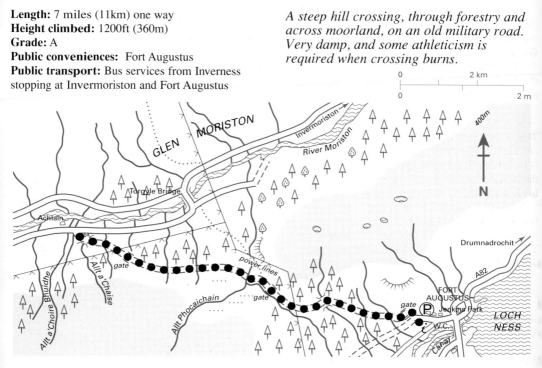

The military roads of the Highlands were built by
the Hanoverians in the 18th-century as part of the
effort to curb the power of the Jacobite clans.
Large stretches are now incorporated into the main
road network; other sections — particularly the
high hill passes, unsuitable for cars — remain as
they were.

The route between Fort Augustus and Glen
Moriston was part of a road — engineered in
1755, but widely used before that by cattle drovers
and the military — to Skye.

This section starts at Jenkins Park. Follow the
road signs from the north end of Fort Augustus.
The road splits, with a group of white houses on
the right hand side of the right fork. Park opposite
these.

Beyond the houses a forestry track goes
through a gate — follow this. A short way beyond
the gate the route to Glen Moriston is signposted
to the right.

The path zig-zags up the hill — at the top of
which there are excellent views of Fort Augustus,
Loch Ness, Loch Oich, the Caledonian Canal and
the Monadhliath Mountains beyond the Great
Glen. It then plunges into dense forestry. Two
miles further on the road emerges onto the moor.
The path is very clear at this point, but disappears
as it approaches Allt Phocaichain. The
Glenmoriston Native Pinewood extends from Allt
Phocaichain down to the main road. Its restart on
the opposite side of the glen is quite visible.
There is no bridge over the burn, which is quite
large and, when in spate, cannot be crossed.

Beyond the burn the track is quite clear, leading
across the moor, down to the edge of the forest,
and then cutting through the trees to the Glen
Moriston Road. This final section includes some
of the original bridges; the largest over Allt
a'Chaise.

18

10 Inchnacardoch Forest

Length: 3¹/₂ miles (5.5km)
Height climbed: None
Grade: C
Public conveniences: None
Public transport: Bus service between Inverness and Fort William; stopping at Fort Augustus

A forest walk through dense, commercial conifer forestry, including a path along the River Oich. Paths good, but damp beside the river.

This route is not unlike every other walk through commercial forestry in the area, but it is considerably lifted by a charming section along the banks of the River Oich, where the river runs in close parallel to the Caledonian Canal.

To reach the route turn left off the A82 Inverness to Fort Augustus road, just north of Fort Augustus, on the road signposted to Auchteraw. The car park is on the left, 1 mile (1.5km) along this road.

The route starts at the back of the car park and joins the river bank soon after crossing Auchteraw burn. The canal — which runs between Inverness and Fort William — is beyond the river, across a narrow partition.

Just after passing a small wooded island, at a bend in the river, the path cuts into the forest and heads back towards the car park. After recrossing the burn it veers left, eventually joining the public road. Walk a short way along this to return to the car park.

At the end of the Auchteraw road there is another car park and further walks through the forest.

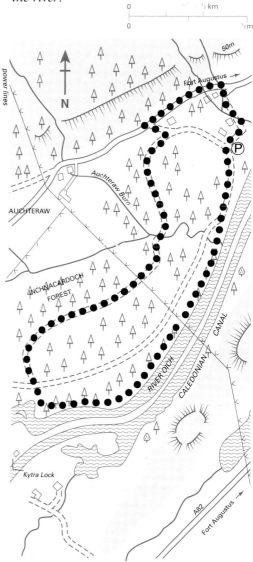

11 Foyers to Whitebridge

Length: 6 miles (9.5km) there and back
Height climbed: Negligible. Steep down to falls.
Grade: B
Public conveniences: Upper Foyers
Public transport: Bus service between Inverness and Foyers

A pleasant walk through forests and farmland by the side of the River Foyers, including a detour to the dramatic Falls of Foyers. Paths of uneven quality.

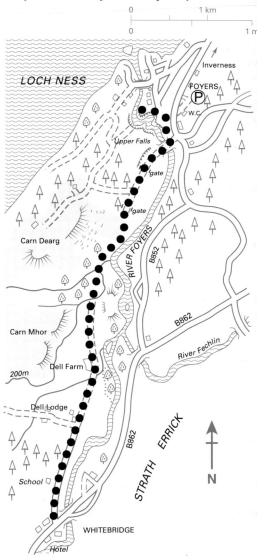

The River Foyers originates in the high moors of the Monadhliath Mountains, to the south, and meanders slowly through the flat land of Strath Errick before falling 450ft (130m) in under a mile, from the upper falls to Loch Ness.

Take the B862 from Inverness to Dores, and then the B852 to Upper Foyers. Park just beyond the shop. There are a great many paths through the conifer woods down the deep gorge to the falls of the river. A potential use for these falls was spotted in 1896, when a hydro-electric power station — one of the earliest in Britain — was built to power the local aluminium works, which at one time produced one-sixth of the total world aluminium production.

The route to Whitebridge starts a little further along the B852, where a path cuts off to the right, across the river. A signpost to Intake House marks the start of this track. The path then continues under the side of a wooded cliff before disappearing into a stand of conifers. Beyond the plantation there is a field. Cross this, bearing to the left of the wooded hill, towards the river. Pass through the wood and, at the far end, cross the burn and head for a gap between two hills. The path is clear from here on, past the farm at Dell and on, down the metalled road to Whitebridge.

Whitebridge was a staging post on General Wade's military road between Inverness and Fort Augustus and, beside the modern road bridge, the original — built over the River Foyers in 1733 — is still standing.

Either return by the same route or double back along the B862 and the B852.

20

12 Farigaig Forest

Length: Up to 2 miles (3km), plus extensions
Height climbed: 350ft (100m)
Grade: C
Public conveniences: Car park
Public transport: Bus service between Inverness and Foyers

A selection of easy routes, of different lengths, through broad-leaved and coniferous woodland, with extensions on quiet country roads.

The hills on the south side of Loch Ness present a steep, unbroken curtain, dropping to the water's edge. Such burns and rivers as penetrate this curtain do so with a mixture of steep gorges and waterfalls. Such a gorge ends at Inverfarigaig, in a garden of natural and landscaped woodland.

From Inverness, take the B862 to Dores, and then the B852 along the lochside. Turn left at the sign for Farigaig Forest Centre.

Beside the car park there is an exhibition centre covering the evolution of the surrounding countryside. In addition there is a leaflet which provides a commentary on points of interest along the paths, and outlines the four available routes, which pass through the broad-leaved woodland of the narrow pass of Inverfarigaig, and the coniferous forestry of the hill to the south of the pass. Among the conifers there are Norway and Sitka spruce, Douglas fir, larch and red cedar — some of which have grown to a considerable height and girth — while the broad-leaved woodland includes birch, alder, oak, ash and others.

Along the routes there are views across Loch Ness to the north, and east to the Monadhliath Mountains.

One possible extension to these paths is to continue beyond Lochan Torr a Tuill and return along the public road (see map). Another alternative is to walk down to the B852 and turn right, across the River Farigaig, and then right again, up an unsignposted road. This road zig-zags to the top of the ridge and gives splendid views of the Pass of Inverfarigaig, and south, across Loch Ness.

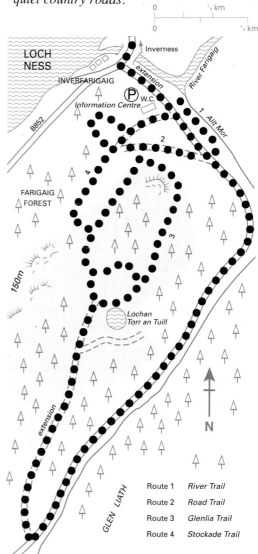

Route 1	River Trail
Route 2	Road Trail
Route 3	Glenlia Trail
Route 4	Stockade Trail

13 Loch Duntelchaig

Length: 5¹/₂ miles (9km)
Height climbed: 200ft (50m)
Grade: B
Public conveniences: None
Public transport: None

A high walk along metalled roads and a rough footpath; by the banks of two lochs; through forestry, woodland and the open moor.

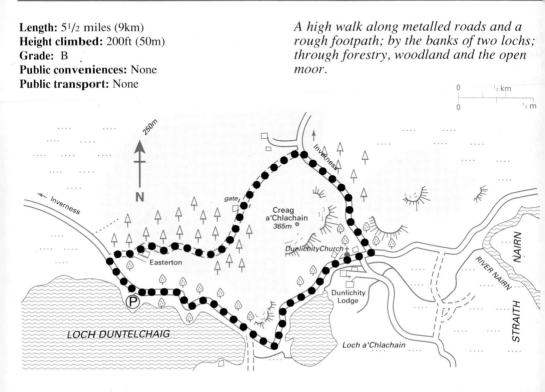

The loch can be difficult to find, but a road map should show an unnumbered road, following the route of an old military road from Inverness to Loch Ashie. Turn left at the junction here for Loch Duntelchaig.

Starting from the parking place by the lochside, walk a short way back along the road and turn right, up the road to Easterton. Keep to the left of the old farm buildings and continue over the hill. This part of the route can be wet in places. The land to either side is planted with conifers. After ¹/₂ mile (0.8km) the trees disappear to give fine views to the north and west over Drummossie Muir. Turn right at the end of the track and walk down the road towards Dunlichty through mixed woodland, with the rugged Creag a'Chlachain to the right. Turn right at the junction.

The church is on a medieval religious site and was rebuilt in the 18th and 19th centuries. The gatehouse, built in 1820 had a rather unpleasant purpose — a guard was stationed here to prevent grave robberies. The churchyard was the burial ground for the chiefs of the MacGillivray clan from Upper Strath Nairn and many others of related clans: Mackintoshes, MacBains, Shaws and MacPhersons.

The road now continues along the edge of little Loch a'Chlachain before cutting right, up the short connecting glen, and skirting the shores of Loch Duntelchaig through a wood of birch and rowan.

To the left at this point is the rocky bulk of Stac na Cathaig *(Hill of the Jackdaws)*: typical of the abrupt hills which punctuate the strange and distinctive landscape of the area.

14 Strath Dearn

Length: 6 miles (9.5km) to Dalarossie and back
Height climbed: Negligible
Grade: B
Public conveniences: None
Public transport: None

A pleasant walk along a metalled public road, through a wide, steep-sided Highland glen with a variety of farmland and woodland.

Strath Dearn is the upper glen of the River Findhorn, where it winds itself into the heart of the massif of the Monadhliath Mountains. The river flows some 50 miles (80km) from the bleak hills north of Laggan to its tidal basin amongst the sand dunes and farmlands of Moray. The Findhorn is a good salmon river and some of these fascinating fish may be seen skimming through the shallow waters, on their way to the head waters of the river to spawn.

To reach Strath Dearn turn off the A9 road — between Inverness and Perth — at the sign for Tomatin, some 16 miles (26km) south of Inverness, and turn left at the first junction. Follow this road through Tomatin and on to Findhorn Bridge. Parking space can be found on the old A9 road bridge over the Findhorn.

Start walking up the road signposted to Coignafearn. The floor of the strath is a flat alluvial plain, typical of the glaciated valleys of the area. It is fertile and supports a mixture of crops and animals. The surrounding hills are steep, and become more so as the road continues up the valley. There is a mixture of natural broad-leaved and coniferous woodland throughout the glen.

About 3 miles (5km) from Findhorn Bridge is Dalarossie Church — a small building, built in 1790 on an older religious site. The church has a lovely position, in a field in a crook of the river.

Turn here to return by the same route or continue for a further 1½ miles (2.4km) up the glen to cross the Findhorn at Dalmigakie Lodge. Then return on the south side of the Findhorn back to the bridge.

15 Brodie Castle

Length: 2 miles (3km)
Height climbed: None
Grade: C
Public conveniences: Car park
Public transport: Bus service between Inverness and Forres

A short walk through farmland and woodland along clear paths and quiet country roads; through the grounds of Brodie Castle — open to the public.

The Brodie family have been living on this spot since before records were begun. The first mention is made in 1249, and a romantic theory traces the family name back to 'Brude' — a common name amongst the Pictish kings who used Inverness as a centre. The present castle was begun in the mid-16th century and has been added to at various times since then. It is open to the public from April to October and the gardens remain open throughout the year. The castle is signposted from the A96 Inverness to Aberdeen road, 6 miles (9.5km) east of Nairn.

There are a number of paths through the castle grounds and gardens, which are notable for their variety of daffodils. For this route, walk west from the castle along the West Avenue — lined principally with copper beech and lime. Cut off the main path and cross the public road.

The shallow pond beyond is entirely man made, and the bird life here — which includes heron, coot and even the occasional visiting osprey — can be viewed from a hide on the south side of the pond.

After circling the pond recross the road and follow the path back down West Avenue, turning right before reaching the castle, down the path to Brodie Village. Walk out of the castle grounds, turn left and walk along the quiet public road to the main entrance, and then up the driveway. A short distance from the gate, up the drive, is the Rodney Stone — a 9th-century Pictish symbol stone with abstract symbols on one side and a Christian cross on the other.

The drive now continues to the car park, and then on to the castle.